Who Was John McCain?

by Michael Burgan

illustrated by John Hinderliter

Penguin Workshop

For my postcard buddy, Mose.
I promise the next book will have
a robot eating a sandwich—JH

PENGUIN WORKSHOP
An imprint of Penguin Random House LLC, New York

First published in the United States of America by Penguin Workshop,
an imprint of Penguin Random House LLC, New York, 2023

Visit us online at penguinrandomhouse.com.

Library of Congress Cataloging-in-Publication Data is available.

Printed in the United States of America

ISBN 9780593383681 (paperback)   10 9 8 7 6 5 4 3 2 1 WOR
ISBN 9780593383698 (library binding)   10 9 8 7 6 5 4 3 2 1 WOR

Contents

Who Was John McCain?

Heavy smoke filled the sky as Lieutenant Commander John McCain flew his A-4 bomber plane over Hanoi, the capital of North Vietnam. The smoke came from large guns on the ground. They were firing at John's A-4 and other US planes soaring over the city at more than five hundred miles per hour.

The United States had been at war with North Vietnam for several years. Now, in October 1967, the Americans were carrying out massive bombing raids on the city of Hanoi. John's job on this day was to drop his bombs on a power plant. It was his twenty-third mission over North Vietnam. He and the other US pilots knew they faced death every time they flew. Despite the risk, they were proud to serve their country.

As John neared the target, the smoke grew thicker. An alarm went off inside his plane. The signal meant that enemy radar was following him. Then another signal went off. John knew that a missile was heading right for him! He was scared, but he was also determined to drop his bombs. A split second after he released them, the missile slammed into his plane. The A-4 spun toward the ground. John pulled a handle to eject his seat out of the plane. A parachute would

carry him and the seat to the ground. But as he
ejected, his body hit part of the A-4 plane. The
impact broke both his arms and his right knee.
He was also knocked out by the force of the
ejection.

Luckily, he landed in water and was quickly alert again. But with his broken limbs, he struggled to inflate his life jacket. Then he blacked out again. When he came to a second time, North Vietnamese soldiers were pulling him out of the water. Others soon arrived and took John away. He was now a prisoner of war.

John McCain spent more than five years as a prisoner. At times, he was tortured. For the rest of his life, he felt the effects of that abuse and the injuries he received after being shot down. But his experience in North Vietnam convinced him that he wanted to continue to serve his country. He decided he could do that by entering politics.

After the war, he represented the state of Arizona in Congress. And in 2008, he ran for president of the United States. John lost the presidential race to Barack Obama, but he continued to serve in Congress. He was known for

his "straight talk"—saying things some people did not like but that he believed to be true. To many Americans, he was a good example of how brave people with strong beliefs can work to make the country better.

CHAPTER 1
A Military Family

The McCain family's history of military service began long before John Sidney McCain III went

John S. McCain Jr.

to Vietnam. He was born on August 29, 1936. His father, John S. McCain Jr., was then serving in the navy and was based in the Central American country of Panama. At the time, the United States controlled the canal that cuts across the country of Panama. American troops protected what was called the Panama Canal Zone.

John III joined his sister, Sandy. A brother,

Joe, was born after him. The McCain children and their mother, Roberta, rarely stayed in one place for long. Lieutenant Commander McCain was often sent to different navy bases.

During World War II, he commanded submarines. After the war, he eventually earned the rank of admiral. His father—John's grandfather—had also earned that top rank in the navy. In fact, members of the McCain family had fought in every US war going back to the American Revolution.

Because the McCains moved so often, young John found it hard to make lasting friends. It didn't help that he also tended to get angry easily. At

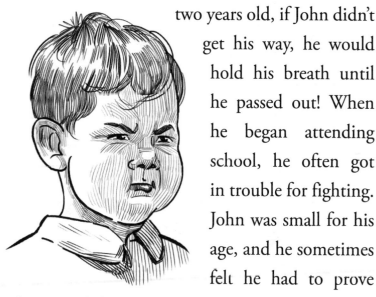

two years old, if John didn't get his way, he would hold his breath until he passed out! When he began attending school, he often got in trouble for fighting. John was small for his age, and he sometimes felt he had to prove how tough he was by starting these fights.

With his father often away for military duty, John grew close to his mother. From her, he learned to find pleasure whenever he could.

Like her, he was outgoing and enjoyed meeting people. And while spending one summer at his grandmother's house, John discovered that he loved to read. Many of the books were adventure tales, and from them John learned that to be a good person, he should treat people fairly.

At fifteen, John entered Episcopal High School, a private school for boys in Alexandria, Virginia. His parents wanted him to get a good high-school education that would prepare John to enter the US Naval Academy. From an early age, John knew he would attend the academy and then become a navy officer, just as his father and grandfather had.

Episcopal High School

John continued to get into trouble at Episcopal. The school had strict rules. Students had to wear a jacket and tie to class, and they

were expected to keep their rooms clean. John broke the rules almost every chance he got. His room was often messy, and he wore jeans with an old jacket. At times, he broke another rule by leaving his room at night to go to nearby Washington, DC. First-year students at Episcopal were called "rats" by the older students. John earned the nickname "worst rat."

Sports helped John win some friends at Episcopal. He was a good athlete and played three sports: tennis, wrestling, and football.

He also became close with one of his coaches and teachers, William Ravenel. In Mr. Ravenel's class, John deepened his love of reading. The teacher also taught John the importance of following the school's code of honor. The code stressed that students should not lie, cheat, or steal. Following the code helped shape a person's character, or how well or badly they acted. Later in life, John wrote, "It is your character, and your character alone, that will make your life happy or unhappy."

In 1954, John graduated from Episcopal and entered the US Naval Academy in Annapolis, Maryland. The rules there were even stricter than they had been at Episcopal, and once again, John got into trouble. He often had to march for miles as punishment for being late to class, not keeping his room clean, or breaking other rules.

John also sometimes struggled with his studies. His favorite subjects were English and history. The academy, though, required many science and math classes—subjects John found difficult. He often asked other students to help him prepare the night before a test. He later said, "I got by, just barely at times, but I got by." In 1958, he left the academy as an ensign—the lowest rank for an officer in the navy.

For the next several years, John learned how to fly planes. Most navy planes fly from large ships called aircraft carriers. John had to learn the difficult task of taking off and landing while the ship moved through rolling waves. Despite the challenges, he loved being a carrier pilot. During the early 1960s, he served on ships that cruised the Mediterranean and Caribbean Seas. John also spent time working on naval bases. In Mississippi, he trained other pilots at a base called McCain Airfield, which had been named in honor of his grandfather.

While in Mississippi, John sometimes traveled to Philadelphia to visit Carol Shepp. They had met in the 1950s when John was at the Naval Academy. In 1965, the couple married. John adopted Carol's two sons from an earlier marriage, Douglas and Andrew. He and Carol then had a daughter, Sidney.

John loved his family and the good times he had with friends at the navy bases. But what he wanted most of all was to fly planes in combat. He got the chance at the end of 1966: He was assigned to the aircraft carrier USS *Forrestal*.

USS *Forrestal*

The ship was soon on its way to Vietnam, where the United States was fighting a major war.

By the summer of 1967, John was thirty-one years old and had earned the rank of lieutenant commander. He had flown five bombing missions over North Vietnam. He almost never got the chance to fly his sixth. One day as he prepared to take off, a missile on a nearby plane accidently launched. It hit the fuel tank of another plane and sparked a fire. John jumped out of his plane and ran through the flames. His

clothes caught fire, but he was able to put it out. Then, the fire blew up a bomb that had fallen from John's plane. The blast knocked him back ten feet and pieces of metal pierced his body. All around him, the fire raged, and more bombs exploded.

The Vietnam War

In 1954, the country of Vietnam in Southeast Asia won its independence from France, and soon after it split into two regions. North Vietnam (Democratic Republic of Vietnam) had a communist government. Under communism, the government owns most businesses. Citizens can't speak freely or elect their leaders. South Vietnam (Republic of Vietnam) was more like the United States—people elected their leaders and could own their businesses. North Vietnam wanted to control the south, which led to a war between the two nations. The United States helped South Vietnam fight communists from the north and within its own country.

By the time John McCain went to Vietnam in 1967, almost five hundred thousand Americans were fighting there. Most US troops left the country in 1973, and the war ended in 1975. North Vietnam

defeated the south and created one communist country. More than fifty-eight thousand Americans and several million Vietnamese died over the course of the war.

John was lucky. He survived the terrible accident on the USS *Forrestal*. But 134 sailors lost their lives, and the ship was badly damaged. Despite the accident, John wanted to fly again.

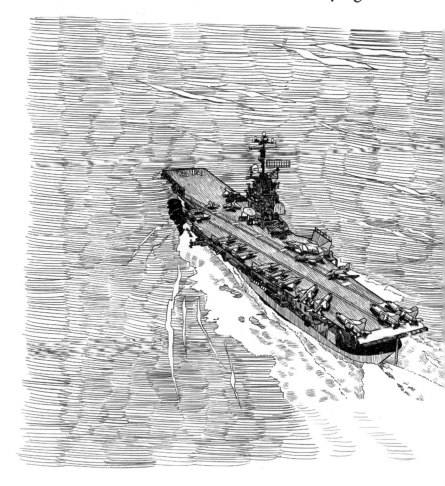

By the fall of 1967, he was on the carrier USS *Oriskany*, once again flying missions over North Vietnam.

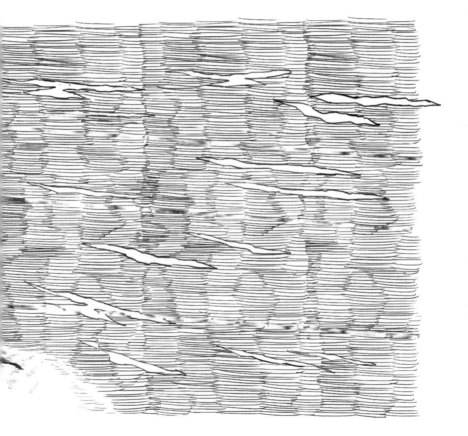

USS *Oriskany*

CHAPTER 2
Prisoner of War

On October 25, John McCain heard about a bombing mission planned for the next day. He begged to be part of it. He had no way of knowing it would be his last flight of the war.

On October 26, after a missile hit his A-4
bomber plane over Hanoi, John reached the
ground and found himself surrounded by local
people. He had been successful in dropping his
bombs over the intended target. But now he was
injured and alone. The North Vietnamese shouted
angrily at him. Their city was being destroyed by
American pilots, like John, dropping bombs on
them. Some of the people hit and kicked him.

He realized that he had been very badly hurt during the crash, and these attacks just made everything much worse.

He was taken to a prison that Americans had nicknamed "the Hanoi Hilton." The name was a joke because the prison was nothing like a fancy Hilton hotel. John spent several days alone in a prison cell. At times, his Vietnamese guards took him to another room and questioned him.

Hỏa Lò Prison, also known as the Hanoi Hilton

They promised him medical care if he told them what they wanted to know about the Americans' military plans. John refused to talk, so his captors beat him, causing even more injuries.

International law requires that nations at war treat their prisoners well. The North Vietnamese often ignored these rules. Some prisoners were even tortured to death. Still, the North Vietnamese wanted to keep most American prisoners of war (POWs) alive. When the war ended, the North Vietnamese hoped they could get the US government to agree to some of their demands. In return, they would release their POWs.

John feared he would die from his injuries and the torture inflicted on him before the two warring countries ever discussed peace. Then, a stroke of luck saved him. The North Vietnamese learned that his father was a navy admiral. They took him to a hospital, where he

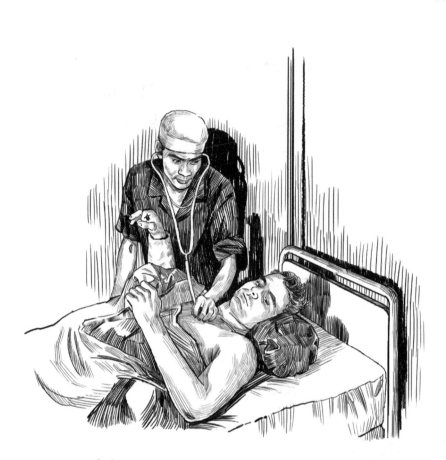

received basic care for his wounds. They also did not beat him as severely as other prisoners. The North Vietnamese wanted to keep John alive. They wanted to show the world that they had captured the son of an important American. They nicknamed him "the Crown Prince."

But keeping John alive didn't mean the North Vietnamese treated him well. Doctors didn't fix his broken arms properly, and his health continued to worsen. He had fevers and infections, and he lost weight, falling to less than one hundred pounds.

John asked to be kept with other American POWs, and the North Vietnamese agreed. At

Norris Overly

a new prison, another POW named Norris Overly helped take care of John. He fed him and helped him move around their cell. Perhaps just as important, John felt better having other Americans to talk to. He became close friends with another cellmate, Bud Day.

After six months as a prisoner, John was still in pain. He needed crutches to walk, and he could not pick up or carry anything. A disease called dysentery made it hard for him to eat, and he was constantly weak and tired. By then,

he no longer shared a cell with Overly and Day.
For two years, John was alone in his cell.

POW Bracelets

More than seven hundred members of the US military were captured and held as prisoners during the Vietnam War. Some Americans wanted to make sure the POWs were not forgotten as the war dragged on.

In 1970, two college students suggested that people should wear a bracelet with the name of a prisoner on it. The wearers promised to keep the bracelets on until the prisoner whose name they wore was released. Some of the bracelets had John McCain's name on them. Over the next few years, five million Americans bought the bracelets.

The money raised covered the cost of making them. Some of the money was also used to raise awareness about American POWs and those who were missing in action (MIA). The US government did not know the location of those men.

The bracelets are still sold today, with the names of those who are still considered MIA. In Tallahassee, Florida, a site honoring POWs and MIAs includes a statue of a POW bracelet that's almost seven feet tall.

The North Vietnamese continued to ask John questions about the US military. He always refused to give them any answers or information, and they sometimes beat him because of it. At one point in 1968, the North Vietnamese offered John his freedom. Even though he was in very poor health, he refused to leave before prisoners who had been captured and imprisoned before him. When they heard this, the North Vietnamese beat him even more fiercely than before. The torture was so bad, John finally agreed to sign a confession saying he had committed crimes with his bombing raids. He didn't believe

he had actually committed crimes, but he felt he had reached a breaking point. The physical pain was just too much.

John's time in prison lasted another four long years. By 1969, his dysentery started to improve. He regained some strength and could even do simple exercises in his cell. At times, he tapped out messages to other prisoners nearby.

They created a code with a certain number of taps standing for different letters.

John discovered some important things during

his time as a prisoner. He realized how much he loved the country he had been sent to fight for. And he thought about being back in the United States. John's next goal was to serve his country in any way he could.

Freedom finally came in 1973. In January, US and North Vietnamese officials agreed to stop fighting. US troops would leave Vietnam,

and the North Vietnamese would turn over the POWs they held. On March 14, John was released. He soon returned home to the United States and his family. Years later, John said that being a prisoner gave him time to think about what was good about his country: "I loved it for its decency, for its faith in the wisdom, justice, and goodness of its people."

Protests against the War

The Vietnam War was unpopular with many Americans. Some who opposed the war were pacifists—they were against *all* wars. Others thought it was wrong for the United States to get involved in Vietnam since South Vietnam was not directly threatened by North Vietnam and the communist government there. Some antiwar Americans thought it was unfair that men who could afford to go to college would avoid serving in the military by doing so. Many young Black and Hispanic men were not enrolled in college at the time. And some Americans thought the money spent on the war should be used to help poor Americans lead better lives.

Protests against the war were held at many colleges and in some cities. The largest protest of the Vietnam War was in November 1969, when as many as five hundred thousand people filled the streets of Washington, DC. Smaller protests were held continuously through 1972.

CHAPTER 3
On to Politics

John McCain and other returning prisoners of war were treated as heroes. John received a lot of attention because of how long he had been in prison and how badly he had been injured. He needed several months of medical treatment to strengthen his body. But some of his injuries never completely healed. He couldn't lift his arms to comb his own hair, which had turned white during his time in prison. And his legs were stiff when he walked. Because of the lasting effect of his injuries, John knew he would never return to combat.

John received a promotion to commander, and during the summer of 1974, he was put in charge of a group of pilots and planes, called a squadron. The squadron was based at Cecil Field in Florida.

Cecil Field

The base trained future carrier pilots. When his time there ended in 1977, John became the navy's liaison (which means their primary contact) with the United States Senate. The Senate is one of the two houses, or parts, of Congress that make the country's laws. The other is the House of Representatives. As the liaison, John tried to educate senators about issues affecting the navy.

John worked as the Senate liaison until 1981. He left the navy that year with the rank of captain. By then, he had divorced Carol and married a second time. With his new wife, Cindy, John eventually had four children: Meghan, John Sidney IV, James, and Bridget, who had been adopted from the country of Bangladesh.

Cindy McCain's father was a successful business owner in Phoenix, Arizona. John went to work for him. He also began thinking seriously

about a career in politics. His time working with
senators had shown him how much lawmakers
can accomplish for their country. In 1982, he
became a candidate for a seat in the US House of
Representatives. A candidate is a person seeking
an elected government position. Most politicians
run in local or state elections before trying to

serve in Washington, DC. John did not have
that experience. But he told Arizona voters that
his time as Senate liaison helped him understand
how Congress worked.

Many voters in the Phoenix area didn't know much about John. He tried to educate them by knocking on doors—twenty thousand of them! That way, he could personally introduce himself to people. In November 1982, John won his race and soon headed to Washington. Every weekend, he flew back to Arizona to meet with voters and be with his family.

The US Government at a Glance

The US Constitution outlines the form of the US government and the country's basic laws. Under the Constitution, the national government is divided into three parts called branches.

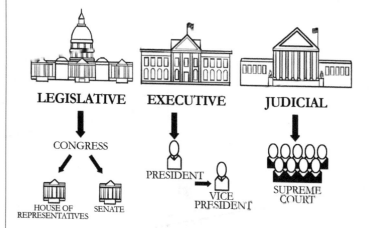

LEGISLATIVE   EXECUTIVE   JUDICIAL

CONGRESS

HOUSE OF REPRESENTATIVES   SENATE

PRESIDENT   VICE PRESIDENT

SUPREME COURT

Congress is the legislative branch, which means it writes bills, which are proposed laws for the country. If the president, as head of the executive branch, approves a bill, it becomes law. The different parts of the executive branch carry out the laws. The nation's courts form the country's judicial branch. Courts decide when a law has been broken. The most powerful court in the United States is the Supreme Court.

John McCain spent most of his adult life working in Congress. In the Senate, he was one of one hundred members. (Each of the fifty states elects two senators.) The House of Representatives has 435 members. (The number from each state is based on its population.) Members of either house of Congress can write a bill. When the bill is approved in both the House and the Senate, it goes to the president, who decides whether to sign a bill, making it a law, or to veto (reject) it.

Ronald Reagan

Ronald Reagan was president of the United States at the time. He, like John, belonged to the Republican Party. John supported many of Reagan's goals, such as strengthening the US military and cutting taxes. He worked hard to help the president achieve those goals.

John won another election to serve two more years in the House in 1984. The next year, he returned to Vietnam and was filmed for a news show that ran on a major TV network. John saw the spot where he had been captured and also the prison known as the Hanoi Hilton. He talked about the pain he and others had suffered. But he also discussed the courage the prisoners had shown during their time in Vietnam. The television show was the first time many Americans saw John as a rising political star.

John returns to Hanoi

John is sworn in to the US Senate

In 1986, John won a seat in the US Senate. He served on the Senate Armed Services Committee, which handles military affairs. He also served on a committee that addresses the needs of Native American tribes. Compared to most states, Arizona has a large Native American population. John worked to protect their interests.

In 1989, John faced the biggest challenge

of his young political career: He was named in a scandal involving an Arizona businessman named Charles Keating who had often donated money to John's election campaigns. John did not break any laws, but his reputation for being an honest politician was damaged. Keating ended up going to jail.

Charles Keating

At times, John became angry with reporters who asked him about the scandal, and his temper flared. To restore his image, he ended his relationship with Charles Keating. And he admitted to mistakes he had made.

The Keating Five

John McCain met Charles Keating in 1981. The two men and their families became friendly. Keating began donating thousands of dollars to John's political races. Keating's businesses included a bank that he owned. The US government suspected the bank had broken the law and was investigating it. Keating asked McCain and four other senators to help him end the investigation. (The other four were Alan Cranston, Don Riegle, John Glenn, and Dennis DeConcini.) They were later called "the Keating Five."

John had taken part in two meetings about the donations. Reporters then found out about all the money Keating had donated to John's campaigns. They also learned that Keating had taken John on vacations on his private jet. By law, John should have paid for those trips, but he

hadn't. In addition, Cindy McCain had a business relationship with Charles Keating. Some people thought it was a case of corruption—a politician using his office to make money and to help his friends.

CHAPTER 4
Becoming a National Figure

A committee of the US Senate investigated John McCain and his role in the Keating Five scandal. It found that he had used "poor judgment." Back home in Arizona, some voters

began to oppose him. But John began to rebuild his reputation during the early months of 1991. In January, the United States and dozens of other countries attacked the country of Iraq, which had invaded Kuwait, its neighbor in the Middle East. President George H. W. Bush sent US troops to the region when Iraq refused to give back the land it had captured from Kuwait.

John supported the US effort to remove Iraqi

troops from Kuwait. Because of his military experience, he was often asked to appear on national television news. On TV, he discussed the fighting in what came to be called the Persian Gulf War. He appeared well-informed about foreign issues affecting the United States. The war ended quickly, with a victory for the United States and its many allies.

Back in Arizona, John was beginning to focus on his next Senate election campaign. Two other people were running for his seat. John, however, easily won. Starting in January 1993, he would go on to serve at least six more years in the US Senate. During that time, he worked to pass laws on matters that were important to him.

One issue was how political candidates spend the money they and their political parties raise. John's goal was to limit how much money

Russ Feingold

large organizations and businesses could donate to individual candidates. The McCain-Feingold Act, addressing this issue, was finally passed in 2002. The law was named for John and the other senator, Russ Feingold, who had written it.

Another important issue for John was the lack of US relations with the country of Vietnam. Since the end of the war in 1975, the United States had no official relationship with its former enemy. Even though he had suffered so horribly as a POW there, by 1994, John thought it was time to begin official communications with Vietnam. Officials in Vietnam had tried to locate some of the US troops still listed as MIA (missing in action)—the soldiers who had never been located after the war. John and some other veterans believed the United States should reward Vietnam for its efforts. President Bill Clinton agreed. In 1995, he sent an ambassador to Vietnam whose job was to represent the United States there. The Vietnamese sent their own ambassador to the United States.

Bill Clinton meets Vietnamese Ambassador Lê Văn Bàng

In 1998, John won yet another election to serve in the Senate. And the next year, he thought it was time to try for something bigger—the US presidency. He was now one of the best-known Republican politicians in the country. He had written a popular book about his time in Vietnam called *Faith of My Fathers*. And a television network made a film about his life. It called him a maverick—someone who doesn't always do what people expect, or want, him to do. John was not afraid to speak out against things other Republicans wanted. Some of them opposed his effort to change the laws regarding fundraising. And at times, he had opposed the ideas of Republican presidents Ronald Reagan and George H. W. Bush.

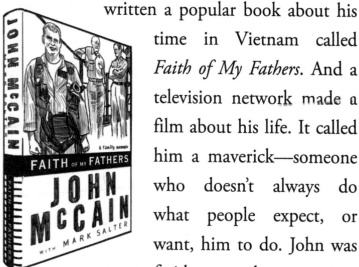

John officially entered the race for president in September 1999. He promised voters he would tell the truth. The bus he and his aides rode in was nicknamed the "Straight Talk Express." News reporters were invited on the bus, too. They enjoyed John's sense of humor and getting to spend so much time with him.

The Republican and Democratic parties

hold primaries (early elections) to choose their candidates. Primaries take place in most states. The first Republican primary in 2000 was held in New Hampshire. John's main challenger in the primaries was George W. Bush, the son of former President George H. W. Bush. The younger Bush had the support of many leaders of the

John McCain and George W. Bush

Republican Party and had raised more money than John. But the senator had spent several months traveling across New Hampshire and meeting voters. He surprised many people when he easily beat Bush there.

The next major primary election was in South Carolina. Bush and his aides realized that John now posed a serious challenge to their campaign. They ran TV ads that said John did not support military veterans, even though he was one! And some people went so far as to spread false rumors saying that John's time as a POW had left him with mental challenges. Bush won the South Carolina primary. He was seen as the most likely Republican candidate for president. More people donated money to his campaign, while John struggled to raise funds. In March, John ended his race for the presidency. But many Republicans still liked him, and he did his best to help other Republicans who were running for Congress.

In the fall of 2000, George W. Bush beat then vice president Al Gore to become the next US president. John McCain returned to the Senate, where he would continue to be a maverick.

CHAPTER 5
Another Race for President

On the morning of September 11, 2001, John McCain was sitting in his office in Washington, DC. He was watching television when he saw a plane fly into one of the Twin Towers, two buildings that were part of New York City's World Trade Center. He and the rest

of the country soon learned that terrorists had hijacked, or taken control of, four large passenger planes. The terrorists then used the planes as giant weapons. They crashed two into the Twin Towers, which were among the tallest buildings in the world. Another flew directly into the Pentagon, the headquarters of the US military, located just outside of Washington, DC, in Virginia. The fourth crashed in a field in Pennsylvania before the terrorists could fly it into another building.

The September 11 attacks killed almost three thousand people. And they led to President George W. Bush sending US troops to Afghanistan, where Osama bin Laden, the leader of the terrorists, lived. Two years later, in 2003, President Bush worked with other nations to invade Iraq. He and his aides believed that Iraqi leader Saddam Hussein had supported the terrorists. They also believed he had weapons that could easily kill many more people using deadly chemicals.

Senator McCain strongly supported what came to be called the Global War on Terror. He went to Afghanistan for the first of several trips in January 2002. US forces and Afghan allies

had quickly taken control of the country, though
they had not captured Osama bin Laden. John
also agreed that Iraq and Saddam Hussein posed
a threat to the United States. As in the 1991

Persian Gulf War, news reporters respected John's views on military actions and foreign relations. They asked for his opinion on how the war was going and what he thought America should do next.

As the wars in Iraq and Afghanistan continued, Americans learned that their government sometimes tortured its prisoners of war. President Bush and his aides wanted information about any planned terrorist attacks. They believed that getting the information was more important than the international laws against torture. Although John supported the wars, he believed torture was wrong. He knew from experience how awful it could be for the prisoners, and it rarely led them to reveal useful information. In 2005, John won support for a law that banned the torture of POWs.

After failing to become the Republican candidate for president in 2000, John doubted

he would run again for that office. But the Global War on Terror changed his mind. He thought the country faced huge challenges. And he believed his military and political experience gave him the skills he needed to lead the country during those difficult times. He also thought he could share an important message with young

Americans—that they should try to serve others and not just look out for themselves. In 2007, he officially said that he was once again running for president.

By then, John had often worked well with Democrats in Congress. They passed laws together, and John had shown he was not afraid to disagree with members of his own party. He was seen as someone who was bipartisan—he believed the two major parties could and should work together on important issues. But not all Republicans wanted to work with Democrats. They didn't trust that John would always pursue Republican goals, including keeping taxes low, stopping immigrants from entering the country illegally, and limiting the power of the national government. John had to convince some Republicans that he did support their goals. But he wanted Democrats and independent voters to know he would remain bipartisan.

The Democratic donkey and the Republican elephant symbols

During 2008, John worked hard to win over voters and to let people see a more personal side of himself. His sense of humor came through later in the year when he appeared on the comedy show *Saturday Night Live*.

John McCain on *Saturday Night Live*

He joked that he could win votes by pretending to be a "sad Grandpa" who didn't have much time left to be president. And some Republican voters valued his experience in Congress. As in 2000, John won the New Hampshire primary. And unlike in that year, he won in South Carolina, too. By March 2008, it was clear McCain would be the Republican candidate for president.

But he knew winning the presidency itself would not be easy. American troops were still fighting and dying in Afghanistan and Iraq. John and some Republicans wanted to send even more troops into the Middle East, but many Americans were getting tired of the wars. They were also tired of the poor and ailing economy. People who had borrowed money to buy homes now couldn't pay back the loans. Several large banks went out of business. And several million people lost their jobs. Voters tended to blame President Bush and the Republican Party for both the long wars and the economic difficulties. John had to convince them that he could solve the problems better than Democratic candidate Barack Obama could.

Obama was a Democratic senator from Illinois. Compared to John, he had little experience in Congress. Some people wondered if he could handle the job of president. But he was young, and he was a good speaker, which appealed to people. He was also the first Black person in the history of the United States to become the presidential candidate for either the Republican or Democratic Party.

But during the campaign, John made history, too. He chose Alaska governor Sarah Palin to be his candidate for vice president. It was the first time the Republican Party had chosen a woman for that role. Then John and Sarah traveled across the country, campaigning. John said in one speech that he would stand on the side of all Americans and fight for their future.

Sarah Palin

Barack Obama (1961–)

Barack Hussein Obama II was born in Honolulu, Hawaii. His Black father was from Kenya and his white mother grew up in Kansas. After graduating from Columbia University, Obama went to Chicago and became a community organizer, where he worked with residents and city officials to improve the lives of the city's poor and people of color. Obama then attended Harvard Law School and began thinking about entering politics.

In 1996, he won a seat in the Illinois State Senate. In 2004, he ran for the US Senate. Before winning his Senate race, he received national attention for the first time when he spoke at the Democratic National Convention. In his speech, Obama stressed that the country should not be divided by race or political beliefs. In 2008, Obama defeated Hillary Clinton to become the Democrats' presidential candidate. He won the election and was sworn in as the forty-fourth president of the United States in January 2009. He was the first Black person to hold the office, and he went on to serve a second term, beginning in 2013.

In the weeks leading up to Election Day, John sometimes gave five or six speeches a day.

By the end of the race, his throat was so sore, he could barely speak. In the end, though, voters wanted a change, and so they elected Barack Obama.

John often said how much he hated losing anything. He was disappointed that he had lost the race for president. But he knew he could still serve his country as a senator from Arizona.

CHAPTER 6
A Respected Voice

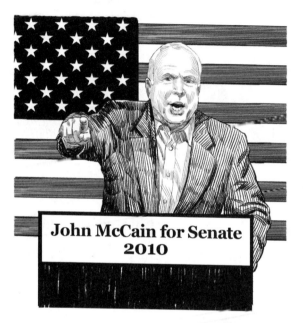

John McCain for Senate
2010

In 2010, John McCain won his fifth term in the US Senate. Members of Congress from both parties did not always agree with him. But they respected his knowledge and his dedication to his country.

John McCain's house in Arizona

Although John worked in Washington and often traveled overseas, he loved going back to his ranch in northern Arizona. It had a creek running through it and tall trees all around. It was the only place where he left behind the demands of being a senator and had time to relax with his family. On the Fourth of July, John and his family and friends celebrated the holiday at the ranch, playing games and having cookouts.

The McCains also owned land on the other side of the creek, which they turned into a protected space for birds. On other trips back to Arizona, John liked to explore the state that he had called home for almost forty years. He enjoyed hiking the Grand Canyon and going rafting on the Colorado River.

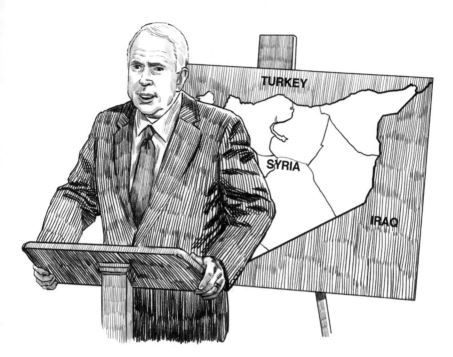

In Washington, though, there was not much time for relaxing. During the Obama presidency, John thought the new president was not strong enough in dealing with other countries that opposed US interests. In one instance, President Obama said he would take military action if the Syrian government used chemical weapons in a war against its own people. The Syrian government then did exactly that. But President Obama did not respond. John later called that the worst decision Obama made as president. He believed the president should have followed through on his promise to use US military force in Syria.

John also opposed President Obama's plan to give more people medical insurance. John knew the US health care system had problems, since millions of Americans lacked insurance

to help pay for medical care. But he thought the government should play a limited role in fixing those problems. He also did not like that the Democrats didn't ask the Republicans to help shape the new health insurance law, called the Affordable Care Act (ACA). It went against his desire to seek bipartisan solutions (those shaped by both parties) to the nation's problems.

A highlight of John's career in the Senate came in 2015. He was named the chair of the Senate Armed Services Committee. In that position, he could help shape the bills that affected the US military. The most important bill spelled out how much money the military would receive each year. John wanted to make sure the military had all the money it needed to carry out its missions. But he hated to see money wasted on expensive weapons. At times, the cost of new planes or ships was billions of dollars more than Congress originally had agreed to pay.

The Affordable Care Act

At the start of the twenty-first century, most Americans got their health insurance through their jobs, while some received it through government programs called Medicare and Medicaid. But in 2009, more than forty million Americans had no health insurance at all. Barack Obama and the

Democrats wanted to help those people. With the Affordable Care Act, larger companies had to offer workers insurance or else pay a penalty. Under the new law, the federal government helped pay some of the cost of insurance offered by private companies.

No Republican member of Congress voted for the ACA. They thought private companies, not the government, should try to fix the insurance problem. But Democrats believed those companies would never act unless the government created the ACA, forcing them to do so.

The ACA did what it was supposed to do. By 2020, the number of uninsured Americans fell to twenty-eight million. The number was still high, but millions of Americans had health insurance for the first time, thanks to the ACA.

Hillary Clinton

In 2016, the country held a presidential election. Hillary Clinton was the Democratic candidate. She had served as first lady when her husband, Bill Clinton, had been president (from 1993 to 2001). She was elected a US senator from New York State in 2000. Under President Barack Obama, she served as the US Secretary of State. In that role, she helped shape America's relations with other countries. Her Republican opponent was Donald Trump. He had made a fortune in real estate, then later appeared on a popular reality TV show. But he had no experience in government. And some

Donald Trump

things he said offended people—including John McCain.

Even before Donald Trump entered politics, he had made fun of John. He said that being captured in Vietnam hadn't made him a hero. Trump later used abusive language to describe John as a "loser" since he had lost his race for president in 2008. John thought that Trump was too extreme in his views on Mexican immigrants.

He also disagreed with Trump's desire to use torture on captured terrorists.

John felt it was his duty to support Trump since the Republicans had  chosen him as their candidate to run for president. But in October 2016, John changed his mind. Reporters discovered that Donald Trump had been recorded making offensive comments about women. John could no longer support him.

That November, John won his sixth term in the Senate. At age eighty, he was one of the oldest and most experienced senators. Donald Trump won his election, too. The difficult relationship between the two men would continue during John's last years working in Washington, DC.

CHAPTER 7
Last Battles

On some issues, John McCain agreed with President Trump. The forty-fifth president wanted to cut taxes on businesses, and McCain agreed. Trump also supported people in Iran who wanted a new government, as did McCain.

John generally supported people, like the Iranians, who wanted greater freedom in their homelands. At times, he wanted to use US military power to help foreigners fight governments that restricted their freedom. Trump, though, was mostly interested in what he called an "America First" policy. He thought the United States should not be involved in foreign wars or work closely with its allies in Europe. John thought this approach was wrong, and he often spoke out against it.

Iranians protest for greater freedom

In Congress, one of the Republicans' big battles was trying to put an end to the Affordable Care Act. John believed that the ACA did have problems. But he thought Americans needed *some* kind of help with their health insurance. He saw that Republican leaders had not come up with a good plan for replacing it.

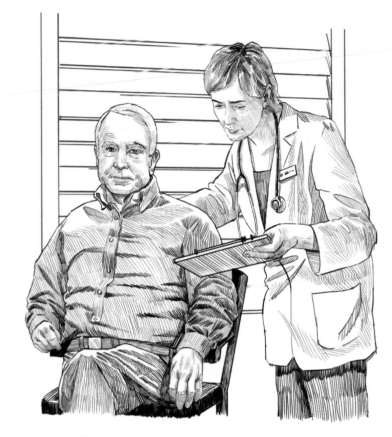

In July 2017, a big vote was coming up in
the Senate on the ACA. Before it happened,
John went for a medical checkup. He had been
feeling tired at times and had some problems with
his vision. The exam showed that John needed
brain surgery. The operation revealed that he had

cancer. The doctors who operated on John told him that it seemed likely the cancer would come back.

Soon news spread about John's illness. His friends—both Democrats and Republicans—reached out to offer support. One was former vice president Joe Biden. His son had died from the same kind of cancer. Biden tried to boost McCain's spirits.

Joe Biden and John McCain

McCain needed to recover from his surgery and then begin treatments for the cancer. But he was not going to let his illness stop him from voting on the ACA. In late July 2017, senators considered a bill that would have gotten rid of parts of the ACA. The Republicans planned to make even more changes in the future. John showed up to vote with a visible scar from his recent operation. He almost started to cry as senators from both parties clapped for him.

He voted yes on a call to debate the Republican bill. But when it was time to vote on whether the bill should be approved, McCain turned his thumb down. He opposed the Republican bill because Republican leaders had tried to rush it through the Senate. He also thought they should have worked with Democrats on the bill. With his vote, the Republican effort to change the ACA was defeated.

Some people thought John's illness led to his

vote that "saved" the ACA. He said no—he just didn't like how the bill had been rushed through the Senate. He hoped both parties would start to work together to address the need for health insurance for everyone.

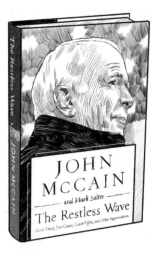

In 2018, John reflected on that vote and his many years of service in Congress in his seventh book, *The Restless Wave*. He focused on his victories in Congress, when he helped pass laws he strongly believed in. He also wrote about his challenges and disappointments, such as losing the 2008 presidential election. By then, the man who had served his country in so many ways knew he was dying. His cancer could not be cured. Still, McCain wrote in *The Restless Wave*, "I'm the luckiest man on earth."

On August 25, 2018, John McCain died at his ranch in Arizona. Politicians from both parties spoke highly about the bravery he had shown in Vietnam. They remembered his efforts in Congress to pass laws that would help the American people. They admired his desire to fight for what he believed in, while also trying to work with politicians who had different ideas.

On September 1, a church service to honor John was held in Washington, DC. Before his

death, he had asked former presidents George W. Bush (a Republican) and Barack Obama (a Democrat) to speak at the service. Even after his death, John wanted Americans to know how much he believed in bipartisan efforts. That message had become especially important as more Americans seemed divided by their political beliefs.

Obama recalled that John was sometimes known for his temper. His face would redden, with "his eyes boring a hole right through you." But at other times, John would stop by the White House just to chat with the man who had beaten him in his race for the presidency. Obama said that he and John "never doubted the other man's sincerity or the other man's patriotism, or that when all was said and done, we were on the same team."

John McCain's style as a maverick sometimes upset people. But he was willing to upset others to do what he thought was right. He showed

great courage both on the battlefield and while
working in Congress. The "Maverick" always
spoke his mind and stayed true to his principles.
And through bravery and hard work, he won the
respect of millions of Americans.

Timeline of John McCain's Life

1936	Born August 29 in the Panama Canal Zone
1958	Graduates from the US Naval Academy
1965	Marries Carol Shepp and adopts her children
1967	Flies bombing missions over North Vietnam and on October 26 is shot down over Hanoi and taken prisoner
1968	Refuses a Vietnamese offer to be released earlier than prisoners who had been captured before him
1973	Released from prison and returns to the United States
1974	Takes command of a squadron at Cecil Field in Florida
1977	Becomes the navy's liaison with the US Senate
1980	Divorces Carol and marries Cindy Hensley
1981	Moves to Cindy's home state of Arizona
1982	Elected to the US House of Representatives
1986	Elected to the US Senate
2000	Runs as a candidate for president but drops out of the race in March
2008	Runs for president as the Republican candidate but loses to Barack Obama
2017	Diagnosed with brain cancer
2018	Dies on August 25 in Arizona; politicians from both parties praise his many decades of public service

Timeline of the World

1929 — The Great Depression begins and millions of Americans lose their jobs and struggle to find food and housing

1933 — President Franklin Roosevelt begins the New Deal to help Americans suffering during the Depression

1941 — Japan bombs the US naval base at Pearl Harbor, Hawaii
— The United States enters World War II

1957 — The Soviet Union launches Sputnik I, a satellite that was the first human-made object to orbit Earth

1969 — The Apollo 11 space mission lands first humans on the Moon

1989 — Animated television show *The Simpsons* is broadcast for the first time

1998 — First Harry Potter book by J. K. Rowling, *Harry Potter and the Sorcerer's Stone*, published in the United States

2005 — Hurricane Katrina strikes New Orleans, killing about 1,800 people and causing more than $100 billion in damage

2007 — Apple sells the first iPhone

2011 — World population reaches seven billion

2013 — The group Black Lives Matter is formed to protest racism and police brutality against Black people

2018 — A record 126 women are elected to the US Congress

Bibliography

*Books for young readers

History.com Editors. "Vietnam War." History. Last modified October 25, 2021. https://www.history.com/topics/vietnam-war/vietnam-war-history.

*Krieg, Katherine. *Congress*. U.S. Government and Civics. Vero Beach, FL: Rourke Educational Media, 2015.

McCain, John, and Mark Salter. *Faith of My Fathers*. New York: Random House, 1999.

McCain, John, and Mark Salter. *Restless Wave: Good Times, Just Causes, Great Fights, and Other Appreciations*. New York: Simon & Schuster, 2018.

McCain, John, and Mark Salter. *Worth the Fighting For: A Memoir*. Random House, 2002.

*Murray, Stuart. *Vietnam War*. New York: DK, 2017.

*Perritano, John. *John McCain: An American Hero*. New York: Sterling Children's Books, 2018.

Povich, Elaine S. *John McCain: A Biography*. Westport, CT: Greenwood Publishers, 2009.

Povich, Elaine S. *John McCain: American Maverick*. New York: Sterling, 2018.

*Rusick, Jessica. *The War on Terror: Then and Now*. North Mankato, MN: Abdo & Daughters, 2021.

"What Is Congress?" Kids in the House. Accessed January 31, 2022. https://kids-clerk.house.gov/young-learners/lesson. html?intID=29.

Website

John and Cindy McCain: Service to Country
https://www.johnmccain.com/

YOUR HEADQUARTERS FOR HISTORY

Activities, Mad Libs, and sidesplitting jokes!

Discover the Who HQ books beyond the biographies